To

_____

From

_____

Date

_____

believe in God's unconditional
and community revealed through the life.
death and resurrection of His Son

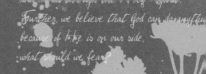

Secret
Strength

Promises of Joy
to Strengthen Your Soul

...inspired by life
EllieClaire com

Ellie Claire® Gift & Paper Expressions
Brentwood, TN 37027
EllieClaire.com
Ellie Claire is a registered trademark of Worthy Media, Inc.

Secret Strength: Promises of Joy to Strengthen Your Soul
© 2014 by Ellie Claire
Published by Ellie Claire, an imprint of Worthy Publishing Group, a division of Worthy Media,
Inc., in partnership with Women of Joy

ISBN 978-1-63326-022-1

Stock or custom editions of Ellie Claire titles may be purchased in bulk for educational,
business, ministry, fundraising, or sales promotional use. For information, please e-mail
info@EllieClaire.com

Compiled by Barbara Farmer

Printed in China

1 2 3 4 5 6 7 8 9 – 19 18 17 16 15 14

Contents

God knows everything about us. And He cares about everything. Moreover, He can manage every situation. And He loves us! Surely this is enough to open the wellsprings of joy.... And joy is always a source of strength.

Hannah Whitall Smith

If God is for us who can be against us?

Romans 8:31 NIV

$\mathcal{Y}$ou are a woman of God with a remarkable destiny, because the One living in you is greater than anything you will ever face in this world. He is your secret stength. He can help you overcome and carry on.

Let go and take God at His Word, trusting that He can and will use even your most painful circumstances for your good and His glory. He will bring joy to your spirit and strength to your heart. Nothing can stop His love for you. You are special, unique, and wonderful.

Remember: God is for you. May that promise fill you with joy and strength.

Debbie Waldrep

Perfect Peace

You will keep in perfect peace
those whose minds are steadfast,
because they trust in you.
Trust in the LORD forever,
for the LORD, the LORD, is the Rock eternal.

Isaiah 26:3–4 NIV

Don't worry about anything; instead, pray about everything.
Tell God what you need, and thank him for all he has
done. Then you will experience God's peace, which exceeds
anything we can understand. His peace will guard your
hearts and minds as you live in Christ Jesus.

Philippians 4:6–7 NLT

Therefore, having been justified by faith, we have peace
with God through our Lord Jesus Christ.

Romans 5:1 NASB

The LORD will give strength to His people;
The LORD will bless His people with peace.

Psalm 29:11 NKJV

Peace I leave with you; my peace I give to you.
Not as the world gives do I give to you.
Let not your hearts be troubled, neither let them be afraid.

John 14:27 ESV

*Wherever you are spiritually, whatever you have been
through emotionally, you are already wrapped in the
Lord's embrace. Held close by nail-scarred hands.
Enfolded in the arms of One who believes in you,
supports you, treasures you, and loves you.*

Liz Curtis Higgs

Strength in His Presence

I have not stopped giving thanks for you, remembering
you in my prayers. I keep asking that the God of our Lord
Jesus Christ, the glorious Father, may give you the Spirit of
wisdom and revelation, so that you may know him better.
I pray that the eyes of your heart may be enlightened in order
that you may know the hope to which he has called you, the
riches of his glorious inheritance in his holy people, and his
incomparably great power for us who believe. That power is
the same as the mighty strength he exerted when he raised
Christ from the dead and seated him at his right hand in the
heavenly realms, far above all rule and authority, power and
dominion, and every name that is invoked, not only in the
present age but also in the one to come.

Ephesians 1:16–21 NIV

Thanks be to God, who in Christ always leads us in
triumphal procession, and through us spreads
the fragrance of the knowledge of him everywhere.
For we are the aroma of Christ to God among those who are
being saved and among those who are perishing.

2 Corinthians 2:14–15 ESV

Let the presence of God invade *you today.*
It's all about Him.

Kari Jobe

Secret Service

*At Joppa there was a certain disciple named Tabitha,
which is translated Dorcas. This woman was
full of good works and charitable deeds which
she did...and many believed on the Lord.*

Acts 9:36, 42 NKJV

As a kid, you had a parent or guardian for feedback. In school, you got a report card. Later, work rewarded effort with promotions or raises...or conversely, the threat of being fired if you didn't perform. No matter what the outcome, at least you knew where you stood, because you had a concrete measure of your effort's value.

But life everywhere else? How can you know if the day-in, day-out service you provide to your kids, spouse, church, friends, and community are worthwhile? Does changing a diaper, making a meal, or writing a letter actually matter in the big scheme of things?

Tabitha's story says yes. She served the Lord with all her heart by sewing garments for others. Making tunics might not sound very glamorous or even noteworthy. But God found her so impressive that after a sickness took her life and left her friends bereaved, he raised her from the dead! Her friends still needed her, and God showed in a most miraculous way that He valued her too. In the end, many believed in the Lord because of this humble seamstress.

Who knows if Tabitha ever got a "thank you" before the big event. Most people only miss kindness when it's no longer there. But God doesn't miss a thing. Every single smile you give, each hug wrapped to comfort, every piece of laundry folded is a fragrant offering of worship to Jesus, the greatest Servant of all. Your reward? An encounter with Jesus that changes you and the world.

Your Father, who sees what is done in secret, will reward you.
Matthew 6:4 NIV

Charity is never lost: it may meet with ingratitude, or be of no service to those on whom it was bestowed, yet it ever does a work of beauty and grace upon the heart of the giver.
Conyers Middleton

God Is Our Refuge

God is our refuge and strength,
an ever-present help in trouble.
Therefore we will not fear, though the earth give way
and the mountains fall into the heart of the sea,
though its waters roar and foam
and the mountains quake with their surging....
The LORD Almighty is with us;
the God of Jacob is our fortress.

Psalm 46:1–3, 7 NIV

You are my hiding place;
You preserve me from trouble;
You surround me with songs of deliverance.

Psalm 32:7 NASB

Hear my cry, O God;
Give heed to my prayer.
From the end of the earth I call to You
when my heart is faint;
Lead me to the rock that is higher than I.
For You have been a refuge for me,
A tower of strength against the enemy.
Let me dwell in Your tent forever;
Let me take refuge in the shelter of Your wings.

Psalm 61:1–4 NASB

*When God has become...our refuge and our fortress,
then we can reach out to Him in the midst of a broken
world and feel at home while still on the way.*

Henri J. M. Nouwen

His Promises Prove True

I love you, LORD, my strength.
The LORD is my rock, my fortress and my deliverer;
my God is my rock, in whom I take refuge,
my shield and the horn of my salvation, my stronghold....
In my distress I called to the LORD;
I cried to my God for help.
From his temple he heard my voice;
my cry came before him, into his ears....
He reached down from on high and took hold of me;
he drew me out of deep waters....
He brought me out into a spacious place;
he rescued me because he delighted in me....
You, LORD, keep my lamp burning;
my God turns my darkness into light....
As for God, his way is perfect:
The LORD's word is flawless;
he shields all who take refuge in him.
For who is God besides the LORD?
And who is the Rock except our God?
It is God who arms me with strength
and keeps my way secure.

Psalm 18:1–2, 6, 16, 19, 28, 30–32 NIV

As you absorb the truth of how much God loves you and grab hold of the promises He has made you, you'll be surprised and delighted as you see yourself being transformed into the vibrant, healthy, complete, beautiful woman you were always meant to be.

Nancy Stafford

You Know Everything About Me

O Lord, you have examined my heart
and know everything about me.
You know when I sit down or stand up.
You know my thoughts even when I'm far away.
You see me when I travel
and when I rest at home.
You know everything I do.
You know what I am going to say
even before I say it, Lord.
You go before me and follow me.
You place your hand of blessing on my head.
Such knowledge is too wonderful for me,
too great for me to understand!...
You saw me before I was born.
Every day of my life was recorded in your book.
Every moment was laid out
before a single day had passed.
How precious are your thoughts about me, O God.
They cannot be numbered!
I can't even count them;
they outnumber the grains of sand!

Psalm 139:1–6, 16–18 NLT

I ust when we think we've messed up so badly that our lives are nothing but heaps of ashes, God pours His living water over us and mixes the ashes into clay. He then takes this clay and molds it into a vessel of beauty. After He fills us with His overflowing love, He can use us to pour His love into the hurting lives of others.

Lysa TerKeurst

God's Great Power

Yours, O LORD, is the greatness and the power and the glory
and the victory and the majesty, for all that is in the heavens
and in the earth is yours. Yours is the kingdom, O LORD,
and you are exalted as head above all. Both riches and honor
come from you, and you rule over all. In your hand are
power and might, and in your hand it is to make great
and to give strength to all. And now we thank you,
our God, and praise your glorious name.

1 Chronicles 29:11–13 ESV

For God is the King of all the earth;
sing to him a psalm of praise.
God reigns over the nations;
God is seated on his holy throne.

Psalm 47:7–8 NKJV

Ah, Lord GOD! Behold, You have made the heavens and the earth by Your great power and outstretched arm. There is nothing too hard for You.

Jeremiah 32:17 NKJV

God is not too great to be concerned about our smallest wishes. He is not only King and Ruler of the universe, but also our Father in Christ Jesus.

Basilea Schlink

Healing Hugs

I was thrust into your arms at my birth.
You have been my God from the moment I was born.

Psalm 22:10 NLT

It started when you were a baby, the comfort of bundled blankets wrapped around you for warmth. Instinctively, you sensed your mother's arms, your father's voice, relaxing in the security of their embrace. From then on, every bump and bruise simply felt better if you could just feel that encouraging hug, the closeness of a loved one lending strength into your world.

But how does God hug His kids? If you reach your arms up, you only feel the seemingly empty air. *I wish God could just give me a squeeze*, you think to yourself.

And then you feel it: That sudden, encouraging text from a friend. That kind smile from your spouse. A clasp around your legs by your little one. God's hugs are coming to you from every direction. From the checkbook that miraculously balanced to the neighbor who stopped by to drop off garden vegetables, God has wrapped your life tightly with His love to bundle you close to His heart.

Realize His presence all around you, and hug Him right back with a heart full of thanks and hands that reach out to help others feel the warmth of God's hugs too.

The eternal God is your refuge,
and his everlasting arms are under you.
Deuteronomy 33:27 NLT

He is everything that is good and comfortable for us.
He is our clothing that for love wraps us, clasps us,
and all surrounds us for tender love.
Julian of Norwich

Contentment

I have learned to be content in whatever circumstances
I am. I know how to get along with humble means, and
I also know how to live in prosperity; in any and every
circumstance I have learned the secret of being filled and
going hungry, both of having abundance and suffering need.
I can do all things through Him who strengthens me.

Philippians 4:11–13 NASB

You're blessed when you're content with just who you are—
no more, no less. That's the moment you find yourselves
proud owners of everything that can't be bought.

Matthew 5:5 MSG

Where you are right now is God's place for you.
Live and obey and love and believe right there.

1 Corinthians 7:17 MSG

The fear of the Lᴏʀᴅ leads to life;
then one rests content, untouched by trouble.

Proverbs 19:23 ɴɪᴠ

Godliness with contentment is great gain.
For we brought nothing into the world,
and we can take nothing out of it. But if we have food
and clothing, we will be content with that.

1 Timothy 6:6–8 ɴɪᴠ

*Contentment is not the fulfillment of what you want;
it is the realization and appreciation
of how much you already have.*

Awesome God

I will exalt you, my God the King;
I will praise your name for ever and ever.
Every day I will praise you
and extol your name for ever and ever.
Great is the LORD and most worthy of praise;
his greatness no one can fathom.
One generation commends your works to another;
they tell of your mighty acts.
They speak of the glorious splendor of your majesty—
and I will meditate on your wonderful works.
They tell of the power of your awesome works—
and I will proclaim your great deeds.
They celebrate your abundant goodness
and joyfully sing of your righteousness.

Psalm 145:1–7 NIV

The Lord is my strength and my song,
and he has become my salvation;
this is my God, and I will praise him....
Who is like you, O Lord, among the gods?
Who is like you, majestic in holiness,
awesome in glorious deeds, doing wonders?

Exodus 15:2, 11 ESV

The highest angelic powers stand in awe of God.
He is far more awesome than all who surround his throne.

Psalm 89:7 NLT

God's quest to be glorified and our quest to be satisfied
reach their goal in this one experience:
our delight in God which overflows in praise.

John Piper

His Renewing Word

For the word of the LORD is right and true;
he is faithful in all he does.
The LORD loves righteousness and justice;
the earth is full of his unfailing love.

Psalm 33:4–5 NIV

You are my refuge and my shield;
your word is my source of hope....
LORD, sustain me as you promised, that I may live!
Do not let my hope be crushed.
Sustain me, and I will be rescued;
then I will meditate continually on your decrees.

Psalm 119:114, 116–117 NLT

All your words are true;
all your righteous laws are eternal.

Psalm 119:160 NIV

You have dealt well with Your servant,
O Lord, according to Your word.
Teach me good discernment and knowledge,
For I believe in Your commandments.
Before I was afflicted I went astray,
But now I keep Your word.
You are good and do good;
Teach me Your statutes.

Psalm 119:65–68 NASB

Not one word has failed of all
the wonderful promises he gave.

1 Kings 8:56 NLT

*Through His Word and our pursuit, His power
and our surrender, the Creator of joy can put His joy
inside of us. He can create in us what we have
not been able to manufacture on our own.*

Angela Thomas

To Be Near God

I am always with you;
you hold me by my right hand.
You guide me with your counsel,
and afterward you will take me into glory.
Whom have I in heaven but you?
And earth has nothing I desire besides you.
My flesh and my heart may fail,
but God is the strength of my heart
and my portion forever....
As for me, it is good to be near God.
I have made the Sovereign LORD my refuge.

Psalm 73:23–26, 28 NIV

God Himself will be with them and be their God.

Revelation 21:3 NKJV

But let all who take refuge in you be glad;
let them ever sing for joy.
Spread your protection over them,
that those who love your name may rejoice in you.
For surely, Lord, you bless the righteous;
you surround them with your favor as with a shield.

Psalm 5:11–12 NIV

*Whenever God thinks of you, he has your best interests
in mind; he has plans to take you further, deeper, and
higher than you ever dreamed. This process begins
when you seek God and spend time with him. Look for
every opportunity to know God.*

Margaret Feinberg

Ripple Effect

*It is God who works in you both
to will and to do for His good pleasure.*

Philippians 2:13 NKJV

It doesn't matter how far you throw it. One minute the water is a mirror, still as stone, reflecting white clouds and blue sky, the tall, colorful trees lining the edges. Then enters the rock. A single shot into the center of stillness, and the picture comes to life. Wave after symmetrical wave rolls out from the epicenter of action, pulsing energy that races out in all directions until it spills onto the lake's sandy shore. It's amazing how one pebble can release so much power.

You, at times, may feel like a simple stone, lining the shore of a place much bigger than you. Powerless, perhaps, to make an impact in this sea of billions of people and places. But remember the ripple effect. When God throws you into the mix He has made, He throws with precision and purpose.

You were made for impact. You, bearer of His glory, will give off an energy that only comes from Him. And it will roll out from you, unstoppable as the waves in the sea. The power of God's love in you is destined for effect—even to the ends of the earth. You will change the face of the world!

Like your name, O God, your praise reaches to the ends of the earth.
Psalm 48:10 NIV

Recognizing who we are in Christ and aligning our life with God's purpose for us gives a sense of destiny.... It gives form and direction to our life.
Jean Fleming

Forever and Ever

From you comes the theme of my praise....
The poor will eat and be satisfied;
those who seek the Lord will praise him—
may your hearts live forever!
All the ends of the earth
will remember and turn to the Lord,
and all the families of the nations
will bow down before him,
for dominion belongs to the Lord
and he rules over the nations.

Psalm 22:25–28 NIV

Grace and peace to you from him who is,
and who was, and who is to come.... To him be glory
and power for ever and ever! Amen.

Revelation 1:4, 6 NIV

If God is for us, who can be against us?

Romans 8:31 ESV

He is the living God and he endures forever;
his kingdom will not be destroyed,
his dominion will never end.

Daniel 6:26 NIV

With God all things are possible.

Mark 10:27 NKJV

*Today Jesus is working just as wonderful works
as when He created the heaven and the earth.
His wondrous grace, His wonderful omnipotence,
is for His child who needs Him
and who trusts Him, even today.*

Hurlburt and Horton

His Powerful Word

For the word of God is living and active and sharper than
any two-edged sword, and piercing as far as the division of
soul and spirit, of both joints and marrow, and able to judge
the thoughts and intentions of the heart. And there is no
creature hidden from His sight, but all things are open and
laid bare to the eyes of Him with whom we have to do.

Hebrews 4:12–13 NASB

With my whole heart I have sought You;
Oh, let me not wander from Your commandments!
Your word I have hidden in my heart,
That I might not sin against You....
I will delight myself in Your statutes;
I will not forget Your word.

Psalm 119:10–11, 16 NKJV

All Scripture is inspired by God and is useful
to teach us what is true and to make us realize
what is wrong in our lives. It corrects us when
we are wrong and teaches us to do what is right.

2 Timothy 3:16 NLT

The Son is the radiance of God's glory
and the exact representation of his being,
sustaining all things by his powerful word.

Hebrews 1:3 NIV

*When we give the Word of God space to live in our
heart, the Spirit of God will use it to take root,
penetrating the earthiest recesses of our lives.*

Ken Gire

No Worries

Can all your worries add a single moment to your life?...
Look at the lilies and how they grow. They don't work
or make their clothing, yet Solomon in all his glory was
not dressed as beautifully as they are. And if God cares so
wonderfully for flowers that are here today and thrown
into the fire tomorrow, he will certainly care for you.
Why do you have so little faith?

And don't be concerned about what to eat and what
to drink. Don't worry about such things. These things
dominate the thoughts of unbelievers all over the world,
but your Father already knows your needs.
Seek the Kingdom of God above all else,
and he will give you everything you need.

Luke 12:25, 27–31 NLT

Do not fear, for I am with you;
Do not anxiously look about you, for I am your God.
I will strengthen you, surely I will help you,
Surely I will uphold you with My righteous right hand.

Isaiah 41:10 NASB

Give all your worries and cares to God,
for he cares about you.

1 Peter 5:7 NLT

Difficulty is inevitable. Drama is a choice.
Anita Renfroe

Leave for a season the remembrance of your troubles
and dwell on the lovingkindness of God,
that you may recover by gazing on Him.

Seek First His Kingdom

Look at the birds of the air; they do not sow or reap or store away in barns, and yet your heavenly Father feeds them. Are you not much more valuable than they? Can any one of you by worrying add a single hour to your life?

And why do you worry about clothes? See how the flowers of the field grow. They do not labor or spin. Yet I tell you that not even Solomon in all his splendor was dressed like one of these. If that is how God clothes the grass of the field, which is here today and tomorrow is thrown into the fire, will he not much more clothe you—you of little faith? So do not worry, saying, "What shall we eat?" or "What shall we drink?" or "What shall we wear?" For the pagans run after all these things, and your heavenly Father knows that you need them. But seek first his kingdom and his righteousness, and all these things will be given to you as well.

Matthew 6:26–33 NIV

*H*unger for God compels us to seek the Lord....
When we seek God with our whole hearts and souls,
he promises to reveal himself to us.

Margaret Feinberg

Speed of Light

Do not forget this one thing, dear friends: with the Lord a day is like a thousand years, and a thousand years are like a day.

2 Peter 3:8 NIV

Did you know that the earth, right now, is spinning 1,040 miles per hour (measured from the equator; it's a good bit slower if you live on the North or South Pole). And you, with all of your busy to-dos, are hurtling through space at breakneck speed, even while spinning like a never-ending top. But we never feel the motion, thanks to gravity—and a very creative God who has a way of handling space and time.

And the facts reveal a deeper truth. Life as we perceive it is not always what it seems. There are forces much greater and stronger than you constantly carrying you through life. God, in His infinite wisdom and love for you, has told you through space—and the time He came into the world—that He has a hidden world of power and purpose surrounding your sensational life.

Today may look like an ordinary day to you, but the God of the unseen world is working faster than the speed of light to make all things work for your good, for every moment of your life in this world to reflect His amazing power and glory. There is no normal. Only spectacular life lived in the knowledge of His mighty power.

When I look at the night sky
and see the work of your fingers—
the moon and the stars you set in place—
what are mere mortals that you
should think about them,
human beings that you should care for them?

Psalm 8:3–4 NLT

The beauty of the earth, the beauty of the sky,
the order of the stars, the sun, the moon...their very
loveliness is their confession of God: for who made
these lovely mutable things, but He who is
Himself unchangeable beauty?

Augustine

Strengthened and Established

I will sing of the LORD's great love forever;
with my mouth I will make your faithfulness
known through all generations.
I will declare that your love stands firm forever,
that you have established your faithfulness in heaven itself....
The heavens praise your wonders, LORD,
your faithfulness too, in the assembly of the holy ones.
For who in the skies above can compare with the LORD?
Who is like the LORD among the heavenly beings?...
Who is like you, LORD God Almighty?
You, LORD, are mighty,
and your faithfulness surrounds you....
Blessed are those who have learned to acclaim you,
who walk in the light of your presence, LORD.

Psalm 89:1–2, 5–6, 8, 15 NIV

The God of all grace, who called you to His eternal glory in Christ, will Himself perfect, confirm, strengthen and establish you. To Him be dominion forever and ever. Amen.... Peace be to you all who are in Christ.

1 Peter 5:10–11, 14 NASB

God wants His children to establish such a close relationship with Him that He becomes a natural partner in all the experiences of life.

Gloria Gaither

My Joy and My Delight

Trust in the LORD and do good;
Dwell in the land and cultivate faithfulness.
Delight yourself in the LORD;
And He will give you the desires of your heart.
Commit your way to the LORD,
Trust also in Him, and He will do it.
He will bring forth your righteousness as the light
And your judgment as the noonday.

Psalm 37:4–6 NASB

I delight to do Your will, O my God.

Psalm 40:8 NKJV

Send out your light and your truth;
let them guide me.
Let them lead me to your holy mountain,
to the place where you live.
There I will go to the altar of God,
to God—the source of all my joy.
I will praise you with my harp,
O God, my God!

Psalm 43:3–4 NLT

The LORD your God is in your midst,
a mighty one who will save;
he will rejoice over you with gladness;
he will quiet you by his love;
he will exult over you with loud singing.

Zephaniah 3:17 ESV

*Our fulfillment comes in knowing God's glory,
loving Him for it, and delighting in Him.
Our joy comes from knowing He delights in us.*

Rest in Him

The LORD is my shepherd;
I shall not want.
He makes me to lie down in green pastures;
He leads me beside the still waters.
He restores my soul;
He leads me in the paths of righteousness
For His name's sake.
Yea, though I walk through the valley of the shadow of death,
I will fear no evil;
For You are with me;
Your rod and Your staff, they comfort me.
You prepare a table before me in the presence of my enemies;
You anoint my head with oil;
My cup runs over.
Surely goodness and mercy shall follow me
All the days of my life;
And I will dwell in the house of the LORD
Forever.

Psalm 23:1–6 NKJV

The law of the LORD is perfect,
refreshing the soul.
The statutes of the LORD are trustworthy,
making wise the simple.
The precepts of the LORD are right,
giving joy to the heart.
The commands of the LORD are radiant,
giving light to the eyes.

Psalm 19:7–8 NIV

When God finds a soul that rests in Him and is not easily moved...to this same soul He gives the joy of His presence.

Catherine of Genoa

God Is Our Help

If you don't know what you're doing,
pray to the Father. He loves to help.

James 1:5 MSG

In the same way, the Spirit helps us in our weakness.
We do not know what we ought to pray for, but the Spirit
himself intercedes for us through wordless groans.
And he who searches our hearts knows the mind of the
Spirit, because the Spirit intercedes for God's people in
accordance with the will of God.

And we know that in all things God works
for the good of those who love him,
who have been called according to his purpose.

Romans 8:26–28 NIV

When you pray, go away by yourself, shut the door behind you, and pray to your Father in private. Then your Father, who sees everything, will reward you.... Store your treasures in heaven, where moths and rust cannot destroy, and thieves do not break in and steal. Wherever your treasure is, there the desires of your heart will also be.

Matthew 6:6, 20–21 NLT

The truth is that God is closest to me when I am suffering. He hears every cry and cares how I am doing. I matter to him. I have not been forgotten. He will not abandon me to the grave. He is here.

Katherine Wolf

In the Gap

Therefore confess your sins to each other and pray for each other so that you may be healed. The prayer of a righteous person is powerful and effective.

James 5:16 NIV

*P*eter's prospects were pretty grim. Authorities had already murdered James, John's brother, for following Jesus. Now Peter was imprisoned by the same hateful people, awaiting a similar fate. All the believers in the city were more than concerned. They wanted to help, but what could they do?

They could pray. They could gather together and ask God to help. And that's exactly what they did. While they huddled together in a house on the other side of town, standing in the gap for Peter, God sent an angel to set Peter free. When Peter arrived at the house where they were praying, they could hardly believe their eyes! Something amazing had just happened, and it had everything to do with God and their prayers.

What is burdening your heart today? What friend or coworker, family member or politician, pastor or missionary could use some help? Don't let prayer be your last recourse or the action for which you apologize, wishing you could help in some better way. Believer, prayer packs more power than any other effort you can give. God has blessed you with this privilege to change the course of history! He has called you to stand in the gap for those who are hurting and in need of him. No authority or child or problem is beyond His reach. Like Peter's friends did, get together with other believers who look to the Lord for strength. Lift up your concerns before God's throne. Intercede for others, just as Jesus does for you. Then watch with amazement what God, your Father, will do through the power of your prayers!

*They all met together and were
constantly united in prayer.*
Acts 1:14 NLT

Praying unlocks the doors of heaven and releases the power of God…. Whether prayer changes our situation or not, one thing is certain: Prayer will change us!
Billy Graham

A New Power

A new power is in operation. The Spirit of life in Christ, like a strong wind, has magnificently cleared the air, freeing you from a fated lifetime of brutal tyranny at the hands of sin and death. God went for the jugular when he sent his own Son. He didn't deal with the problem as something remote and unimportant. In his Son, Jesus, he personally took on the human condition, entered the disordered mess of struggling humanity in order to set it right once and for all....

What the law code asked for but we couldn't deliver is accomplished as we, instead of redoubling our own efforts, simply embrace what the Spirit is doing in us.... Those who trust God's action in them find that God's Spirit is in them—living and breathing God!

Romans 8:2–6 MSG

God is working in you, giving you the desire
and the power to do what pleases him.

Philippians 2:13 NLT

God has promised us even more than His own Son.
He's promised us power through the Spirit—
power that will help us do all that He asks of us.

Joni Eareckson Tada

Everything You Need

Don't fuss about what's on the table at mealtimes
or if the clothes in your closet are in fashion. There is far
more to your inner life than the food you put in your
stomach, more to your outer appearance than the clothes
you hang on your body. Look at the ravens, free and
unfettered, not tied down to a job description, carefree
in the care of God. And you count far more.

Luke 12:22–24 MSG

His divine power has given us everything we need for a godly
life through our knowledge of him who called us by his own
glory and goodness. Through these he has given us his very
great and precious promises.

2 Peter 1:3–4 NIV

God will generously provide all you need.
Then you will always have everything you need
and plenty left over to share with others.

2 Corinthians 9:8 NLT

I am like a luxuriant fruit tree.
Everything you need is to be found in me.

Hosea 14:8 MSG

We've all had experiences of pain and rejection.
The world has at times pushed us away, judging us or
the ones we love based on our appearance or popularity
or social acceptance. But God sees our hearts.
He knows our needs...and draws us near.

Nancy Stafford

Fresh Hope

God....rekindles burned-out lives with fresh hope, restoring
dignity and respect to their lives—a place in the sun! For the
very structures of earth are God's;
he has laid out his operations on a firm foundation.

1 Samuel 2:7–8 MSG

You are my hope; O Lord God,
You are my confidence from my youth.
By You I have been sustained from my birth;
You are He who took me from my mother's womb;
My praise is continually of You.

Psalm 71:5–6 NASB

Now may the God of hope fill you
with all joy and peace in believing.

Romans 15:13 NKJV

We can rejoice, too, when we run into problems and trials,
for we know that they help us develop endurance.
And endurance develops strength of character,
and character strengthens our confident hope of salvation.
And this hope will not lead to disappointment.
For we know how dearly God loves us.

Romans 5:3–5 NLT

*God specializes in things fresh and firsthand....
His plans for you this year may outshine those
of the past.... He's prepared to fill your days
with reasons to give Him praise.*

Joni Eareckson Tada

God Is Enough

It is God who arms me with strength,
And makes my way perfect....
You have also given me the shield of Your salvation;
Your right hand has held me up,
Your gentleness has made me great.
You enlarged my path under me,
So my feet did not slip.

Psalm 18:32–33, 35–36 NKJV

He said to me, "My grace is sufficient for you,
for my power is made perfect in weakness."
Therefore I will boast all the more gladly of my weaknesses,
so that the power of Christ may rest upon me.

2 Corinthians 12:9 ESV

It is not that we think we are qualified to do anything on our own. Our qualification comes from God. He has enabled us to be ministers of his new covenant. This is a covenant not of written laws, but of the Spirit. The old written covenant ends in death; but under the new covenant, the Spirit gives life.

2 Corinthians 3:5–6 NLT

God has been gracious to me and I have all I need.

Genesis 33:11 NIV

Nothing can separate you from His love, absolutely nothing.... God is enough for time, and God is enough for eternity. God is enough!

Hannah Whitall Smith

Standing Tall

When you walk through the fire, you will not be
burned; the flames will not set you ablaze.
For I am the LORD your God,
the Holy One of Israel, your Savior.

Isaiah 43:2–3 NIV

*T*he giant sequoia trees off California's coast have a secret
to their unprecedented success as the tallest trees in the
world. Some standing as tall as a twenty-five-story building,
their massive trunks stretch over thirty feet in diameter. But
that's where you find the secret's source. Soot darkens wide
swaths of bark, harking back to the fiery blaze that burned
across its path not long ago.

Oddly, fire—the one element that would seem to threat-
en their existence—actually aids their exponential growth.
Over time, forest foliage, vines, and underbrush block out
the sun and rain necessary for the sequoia's roots. Only a forest fire can clear the debris to create a way for greater growth.

God, the maker of the great sequoia, works the same
wonder in the lives of His people. You may not see any
point to the pain you have experienced in life. But somehow,

through suffering, God clears away the wrong thoughts and distractions that make us spiritually malnourished. Though the heat may be hard to endure, keep standing strong. God is clearing the way for you to grow strong and tall, flourishing in His unfailing love.

Since we are receiving a kingdom that cannot be shaken, let us be thankful, and so worship God acceptably with reverence and awe, for our "God is a consuming fire."

Hebrews 12:28–29 NIV

I believe that God meant for life to take our breath away, sometimes because of the sheer joy of it all and sometimes because of the severe pain. To choose living over pretending means that we will know both.

Angela Thomas

A Dependable Friend

I will sing of the LORD's great love forever;
with my mouth I will make your faithfulness known
through all generations.
I will declare that your love stands firm forever,
that you have established your faithfulness in heaven itself....
The heavens praise your wonders, LORD,
your faithfulness too, in the assembly of the holy ones....
Who is like you, LORD God Almighty?
You, LORD, are mighty, and your faithfulness surrounds you.

Psalm 89:1–2, 5, 8 NIV

May God himself, the God who makes everything holy and
whole, make you holy and whole, put you together—spirit,
soul, and body—and keep you fit for the coming of our
Master, Jesus Christ. The One who called you is completely
dependable. If he said it, he'll do it!

1 Thessalonians 5:23–24 MSG

I pray that God, the source of hope, will fill you completely
with joy and peace because you trust in him.
Then you will overflow with confident hope through the
power of the Holy Spirit.... And now may God,
who gives us his peace, be with you all. Amen.

Romans 15:13, 33 NLT

*The more we depend on God
the more dependable we find He is.*
Cliff Richard

Daily Provisions

May the LORD answer you when you are in distress;
may the name of the God of Jacob protect you.
May he send you help from the sanctuary
and grant you support from Zion....
May he give you the desire of your heart
and make all your plans succeed.
May we shout for joy over your victory
and lift up our banners in the name of our God.
May the LORD grant all your requests.

Psalm 20:1–2, 4–5 NIV

You take care of the earth and water it,
making it rich and fertile....
You soften the earth with showers
and bless its abundant crops.
You crown the year with a bountiful harvest;
even the hard pathways overflow with abundance.
The grasslands of the wilderness become a lush pasture,
and the hillsides blossom with joy.
The meadows are clothed with flocks of sheep,
and the valleys are carpeted with grain.
They all shout and sing for joy!

Psalm 65:9–13 NLT

*He is the Source. Of everything. Strength for your day.
Wisdom for your task. Comfort for your soul. Grace for
your battle. Provision for each need. Understanding
for each failure. Assistance for every encounter.*

Jack Hayford

Fulfilled Promises

Remember your promise to me;
it is my only hope.
Your promise revives me;
it comforts me in all my troubles....
Your eternal word, O Lord,
stands firm in heaven.
Your faithfulness extends to every generation,
as enduring as the earth you created.
Your regulations remain true to this day,
for everything serves your plans....
Your promises have been thoroughly tested;
that is why I love them so much.

Psalm 119:49–50, 89–91, 140 NLT

Not one word of all the good words which the Lord your
God spoke concerning you has failed; all have been fulfilled
for you, not one of them has failed.

Joshua 23:14 NASB

The fulfillment of God's promise depends entirely on
trusting God and his way, and then simply embracing him
and what he does. God's promise arrives as pure gift.

Romans 4:16 msg

You faithfully answer our prayers with awesome deeds,
O God our savior.
You are the hope of everyone on earth,

Psalm 65:5 nlt

By day the LORD directs his love,
at night his song is with me—
a prayer to the God of my life.

Psalm 42:8 niv

We may...depend upon God's promises,
for...He will be as good as His word.
Matthew Henry

Watching Over You

Whoever dwells in the shelter of the Most High
will rest in the shadow of the Almighty.
I will say of the LORD, "He is my refuge and my fortress,
my God, in whom I trust."...
If you say, "The LORD is my refuge,"
and you make the Most High your dwelling,
no harm will overtake you,
no disaster will come near your tent.
For he will command his angels concerning you
to guard you in all your ways.

Psalm 91:1–2, 9–11 NIV

The LORD says, "I will guide you along
the best pathway for your life.
I will advise you and watch over you."

Psalm 32:8 NLT

But you, O LORD, are a shield around me;
you are my glory, the one who holds my head high.
I cried out to the LORD,
and he answered me from his holy mountain.
I lay down and slept,
yet I woke up in safety,
for the LORD was watching over me.

Psalm 3:3–5 NLT

*God is constantly taking knowledge of me
in love and watching over me for my good.*

J. I. Packer

Race Runner

Those who hope in the LORD will renew their strength.
They will soar on wings like eagles; they will run and
not grow weary, they will walk and not be faint.

Isaiah 40:31 NIV

*H*ave you ever run or exercised so hard that your legs start to burn? Determined to reach your fitness goal, you press on. But suddenly your limbs seem heavier, awkward, hard to move. Then you realize, you're wiped out. Water and a little breather are required if you want to get back in the game.

Sometimes service for God can feel that way. You start off marriage, the parenting years, maybe a volunteer position with all the energy and enthusiasm in the world. But as you pour yourself out for others, you start to feel the drain. Looking around, you notice not many bother to reciprocate or even appreciate what you're giving. You begin to wonder if it's worth it.

Don't lose sight of the finish line. You are running the race God has given you. Though others may not notice your sacrifice, God does. You are not running in vain, you are running for the prize—Jesus, Himself. As you learn to lean into Him for strength, His living water refreshes your soul.

In time, sometimes a long time, you start to see your perseverance pay off. God promises that you will reap a harvest if you just don't give up.

So if you're soul is tired, take some time to drink in God's life-giving water. Rest until you catch your breath. But don't walk away from the race. Restore your hope in the Lord and watch Him renew your strength.

Let us run with endurance the race that is set before us, looking to Jesus, the founder and perfecter of our faith.
Hebrews 12:1–2 ESV

By reading of Scripture I am so renewed that all nature seems renewed…. The sky seems to be…a cooler blue, the trees a deeper green…and the whole world is charged with the glory of God.
Thomas Merton

Light in the Darkness

In the beginning was the Word, and the Word was with God, and the Word was God. He was with God in the beginning. Through him all things were made; without him nothing was made that has been made. In him was life, and that life was the light of all mankind. The light shines in the darkness, and the darkness has not overcome it.

John 1:1–4 NIV

Jesus spoke to them, saying, "I am the light of the world. Whoever follows me will not walk in darkness, but will have the light of life."

John 8:12 ESV

For God, who said, "Let light shine out of darkness,"
made his light shine in our hearts to give us the light of the
knowledge of God's glory displayed in the face of Christ.
But we have this treasure in jars of clay to show that this
all-surpassing power is from God and not from us.

2 Corinthians 4:6–7 NIV

*Open wide the windows of our spirits
and fill us full of light; open wide the door of our
hearts, that we may receive and entertain
You with all our powers of adoration.*

Christina Rossetti

Bought with a Price

Don't be afraid, I've redeemed you.
I've called your name. You're mine.
When you're in over your head, I'll be there with you.
When you're in rough waters, you will not go down.
When you're between a rock and a hard place,
it won't be a dead end—
Because I am GOD, your personal God,
The Holy of Israel, your Savior.
I paid a huge price for you...!
That's how much you mean to me!
That's how much I love you!

Isaiah 43:1–4 MSG

For you know that it was not with perishable things
such as silver or gold that you were redeemed from
the empty way of life...but with the precious blood of Christ,
a lamb without blemish or defect.

1 Peter 1:18–19 NIV

Do you not know that your body is a temple of the Holy
Spirit within you, whom you have from God?
You are not your own, for you were bought with a price.
So glorify God in your body.

1 Corinthians 6:19–20 ESV

*You are in the Beloved...therefore infinitely dear
to the Father, unspeakably precious to Him.*

Norman F. Dowty

Renewed Every Day

Though our bodies are dying, our spirits are being renewed every day. For our present troubles are small and won't last very long. Yet they produce for us a glory that vastly outweighs them and will last forever! So we don't look at the troubles we can see now; rather, we fix our gaze on things that cannot be seen. For the things we see now will soon be gone, but the things we cannot see will last forever.

2 Corinthians 4:16–18 NLT

Now to Him who is able to keep you from stumbling, and to make you stand in the presence of His glory blameless with great joy, to the only God our Savior, through Jesus Christ our Lord, be glory, majesty, dominion and authority, before all time and now and forever. Amen.

Jude 1:24–25 NASB

Create in me a pure heart, O God,
and renew a steadfast spirit within me....
Restore to me the joy of your salvation
and grant me a willing spirit, to sustain me.

Psalm 51:10, 12 NIV

*Be still, and in the quiet moments, listen to the voice
of your heavenly Father. His words can renew your
spirit...no one knows you and your needs like He does.*

Janet L. Smith

My Personal Guide

I'll take the hand of those who don't know the way, who can't see where they're going. I'll be a personal guide to them, directing them through unknown country. I'll be right there to show them what roads to take, make sure they don't fall into the ditch. These are the things I'll be doing for them— sticking with them, not leaving them for a minute.

Isaiah 42:16 MSG

Show me your ways, LORD,
teach me your paths.
Guide me in your truth and teach me,
for you are God my Savior,
and my hope is in you all day long.

Psalm 25:4–5 NIV

Whether you turn to the right or to the left, your ears will hear a voice behind you, saying, "This is the way; walk in it."

Isaiah 30:21 NIV

The LORD is good and does what is right;
he shows the proper path to those who go astray.
He leads the humble in doing right,
teaching them his way.

Psalm 25:8–9 NLT

We have ample evidence that the Lord is able to guide.
The promises cover every imaginable situation.
All we need to do is to take the hand He stretches out.

Elisabeth Elliot

A True Friend

Then Jonathan made a covenant with David,
because he loved him as his own soul.
And Jonathan stripped himself of the robe that
was on him and gave it to David, and his armor,
and even his sword and his bow and his belt.

1 Samuel 18:3–4 ESV

*T*he tabloids today are filled with stories of treachery. Just when a celebrity's life couldn't seem better, a trusted friend betrays a family secret, or cheats with someone else. It's a wonder why the not-so-famous people pay good money to read them.

Maybe it's to add drama to an average life. Or the shock value of scandal. But maybe it's because it makes us remember that fame isn't all glory, and good friends are gifts who can't be bought.

And maybe that's why the friendship between Jonathan and David is so amazing. Jonathan, son of King Saul, was poised to be Israel's next king. But when he heard David, a common Israelite speak before his father, Jonathan was more than moved. Shockingly, he committed to always be David's friend, even if it meant giving David his throne. Proving his loyalty, he removed his royal armor and gave it to David, a graphic picture of Jonathan's determination to do whatever it took to make David prosper.

Such loyalty hardly computes. Does anyone like that exist in the world today?

The friend who may have given you this book says yes. And you may have been that good friend, giving of yourself to better others. Moreover, Scripture reminds you that you also have a Friend who sticks closer than a brother. Like Jonathan, Jesus gave up His royal robes to cover you in righteousness and call you His forever friend. It is His steadfast love that strengthens you to become a faithful friend to others.

There is a friend who sticks closer than a brother.

Proverbs 18:24 ESV

He doesn't leave you during the night.
He doesn't get busy and forget you are here
facing challenges. He is with you!

Jan Silvious

A New Wardrobe

Now you're dressed in a new wardrobe. Every item of your
new way of life is custom-made by the Creator, with his label
on it. All the old fassions are now obsolete.... From now
on everyone is defined by Christ, everyone is included in
Christ. So, chosen by God for this new life of love, dress in
the wardrobe God picked out for you: compassion, kindness,
humility, quiet strength, discipline. Be even-tempered,
content with second place, quick to forgive an offense.
Forgive as quickly and completely as the Master forgave you.
And regardless of what else you put on, wear love. It's your
basic, all-purpose garment. Never be without it.

Colossians 3:10–14 MSG

So in Christ Jesus you are all children of God through faith,
for all of you who were baptized into Christ have clothed
yourselves with Christ.

Galatians 3:26–27 NIV

You have turned for me my mourning into dancing;
You have put off my sackcloth and clothed me with gladness.

Psalm 30:11 NKJV

She is clothed with strength and dignity;
she can laugh at the days to come.

Proverbs 31:25 NIV

God shines brightly through the soul that is wholly devoted to Him. Satisfied in Him. Trusting in Him. Delighting in Him.

Angela Thomas

Power to Accomplish

Dear brothers and sisters, we can't help but thank God for
you, because your faith is flourishing and your love for one
another is growing....
We keep on praying for you, asking our God to enable you
to live a life worthy of his call. May he give you the power to
accomplish all the good things your faith prompts you to do.
Then the name of our Lord Jesus will be honored because of
the way you live, and you will be honored along with him.
This is all made possible because of the grace of our God
and Lord, Jesus Christ.

2 Thessalonians 1:3, 11–12 NLT

Exercise daily in God.... Workouts in the gymnasium
are useful, but a disciplined life in God is far more so,
making you fit both today and forever.
You can count on this. Take it to heart.

1 Timothy 4:7–8 MSG

A generous person will prosper;
whoever refreshes others will be refreshed.

Proverbs 11:25 NIV

*To love God, to serve Him because we love Him,
is...our highest happiness.... Love makes all labor light.
We serve with enthusiasm where we love with sincerity.*

Hannah More

The Lord Has Been Good

I love the LORD, for he heard my voice;
he heard my cry for mercy.
Because he turned his ear to me,
I will call on him as long as I live....
I was overcome by distress and sorrow.
Then I called on the name of the LORD....
The LORD is gracious and righteous;
our God is full of compassion.
The LORD protects the unwary;
when I was brought low, he saved me.
Return to your rest, my soul,
for the LORD has been good to you.
For you, LORD, have delivered me from death,
my eyes from tears,
my feet from stumbling,
that I may walk before the LORD
in the land of the living.

Psalm 116:1–9 NIV

The Lord remembers us and will bless us:
He will bless his people Israel,
he will bless the house of Aaron,
he will bless those who fear the Lord—
small and great alike.
May the Lord cause you to flourish,
both you and your children.
May you be blessed by the Lord,
the Maker of heaven and earth.

Psalm 115:12–15 NIV

The Lord's goodness surrounds us at every moment.
I walk through it almost with difficulty,
as through thick grass and flowers.

R. W. Barber

A Sense of Destiny

The God who made the world and everything in it is the
Lord of heaven and earth and does not live in temples built
by human hands. And he is not served by human hands,
as if he needed anything. Rather, he himself gives everyone
life and breath and everything else.... God did this
so that they would seek him and perhaps reach out for him
and find him, though he is not far from any one of us.
"For in him we live and move and have our being."

Acts 17:24–25, 27–28 NIV

The LORD is gracious and merciful,
slow to anger and abounding in steadfast love.
The LORD is good to all,
and his mercy is over all that he has made....
The LORD is faithful in all his words,
and kind in all his works.

Psalm 145:8–9, 13 ESV

*For from Him and through Him and to Him are all
things. To Him be the glory forever. Amen.*

Romans 11:36 NASB

Keep Connected

I am the vine, you are the branches.
He who abides in Me, and I in him, bears much fruit;
for without Me you can do nothing.

John 15:5 NKJV

Would you ever get mad at your three-year-old because he wouldn't help you fill out your tax forms? How absurd! No one would have such impossible expectations. They would go to someone who was trained and qualified for such work.

But do you ever get mad at yourself because you failed in an area you thought you should be able to handle by now, like that temper? That fly-off-the-handle mouth? That persistent worry? You confess and try harder. Then harder. Harder still, until you conclude it's no use. That sin is just going to stay.

Like trees in the wind, Jesus' words in John 15 remind you of a strength far greater than your own. He asks you to consider branches, and their ability to produce fruit. Dry and lifeless on the ground, they are powerless to produce anything. Connected to the vine, growth is inevitable. Just like you wouldn't expect a child to conjure wisdom outside his capacity, so you should rest from your frustration with sin, realizing you are powerless on your own to defeat it. Plug into Christ. Draw nourishment from His presence. Let His Word and Spirit renew your mind as you praise Him for His faithfulness. In time, you will see fruit. Not the contrived kind that doesn't last, but the genuine, life-giving sweetness that comes and stays through Christ.

They are like trees planted along the riverbank,
bearing fruit each season.
Their leaves never wither,
and they prosper in all they do.
Psalm 1:3 NLT

Should we feel...discouraged, a simple movement of
heart toward God will renew our powers. Whatever
He may demand of us, He will give us...the strength
and courage that we need.
François Fénelon

Our Help and Shield

I will lift up my eyes to the hills—
From whence comes my help?
My help comes from the LORD,
Who made heaven and earth.
He will not allow your foot to be moved;
He who keeps you will not slumber.
Behold, He who keeps Israel
Shall neither slumber nor sleep.
The LORD is your keeper;
The LORD is your shade at your right hand.
The sun shall not strike you by day,
Nor the moon by night.
The LORD shall preserve you from all evil;
He shall preserve your soul.
The LORD shall preserve your going out and your coming in
from this time forth, and even forevermore.

Psalm 121:1–8 NKJV

Our soul waits for the Lord;
he is our help and our shield.
For our heart is glad in him,
because we trust in his holy name.
Let your steadfast love, O Lord, be upon us,
even as we hope in you.

Psalm 33:20–22 esv

We have a Father in heaven who is almighty, who loves His children as He loves His only-begotten Son, and whose very joy and delight it is to...help them at all times and under all circumstances.

George Mueller

Love Much, Love Well

I pray that your love will overflow more and more,
and that you will keep on growing in knowledge
and understanding. For I want you to understand
what really matters, so that you may live pure and blameless
lives until the day of Christ's return.

Philippians 1:9–10 NLT

I thank my God every time I remember you. In all my
prayers for all of you, I always pray with joy because of your
partnership in the gospel from the first day until now, being
confident of this, that he who began a good work in you will
carry it on to completion until the day of Christ Jesus.

Philippians 1:3–6 NIV

Oh! Teach us to live well!
Teach us to live wisely and well!...
Surprise us with love at daybreak;
then we'll skip and dance all the day long.

Psalm 90:12, 14 MSG

*Remember you are very special to God as His precious
child. He has promised to complete the good work He
has begun in you. As you continue to grow in Him,
He will teach you to be a blessing to others.*

Gary Smalley and John Trent

Safe Haven

He rescues you from hidden traps,
shields you from deadly hazards.
His huge outstretched arms protect you—
under them you're perfectly safe;
his arms fend off all harm....
"If you'll hold on to me for dear life," says GOD,
"I'll get you out of any trouble.
I'll give you the best of care
if you'll only get to know and trust me.
Call me and I'll answer, be at your side in bad times."

Psalm 91:3–6, 14–15 MSG

You are God, my only safe haven.

Psalm 43:2 NLT

They cried out to the LORD in their trouble,
And he brought them out of their distress.
He stilled the storm to a whisper;
the waves of the sea were hushed.
They were glad when it grew calm,
and he guided them to their desired haven.

Psalm 107:28–30 NIV

Only Christ Himself, who slept in the boat in the storm and then spoke calm to the wind and waves, can stand beside us when we are in a panic and say to us Peace. It will not be explainable. It transcends human understanding. And there is nothing else like it in the whole wide world.

Elisabeth Elliot

The Apple of His Eye

Who shall separate us from the love of Christ? Shall trouble
or hardship or persecution or famine or nakedness or
danger or sword?... No, in all these things we are more than
conquerors through him who loved us. For I am convinced
that neither death nor life, neither angels nor demons,
neither the present nor the future, nor any powers,
neither height nor depth, nor anything else in all creation,
will be able to separate us from the love of God
that is in Christ Jesus our Lord.

Romans 8:35, 37–39 NIV

Show me the wonders of your great love,
you who save by your right hand
those who take refuge in you from their foes.
Keep me as the apple of your eye;
hide me in the shadow of your wings.

Psalm 17:7–8 NIV

As soon as I pray, you answer me;
you encourage me by giving me strength....
The LORD will work out his plans for my life—
for your faithful love, O LORD, endures forever.

Psalm 138:3, 8 NLT

*Despite the heartache you have over the choices
you have made, it's never too late for Him
to sculpt you into something beautiful.*

Angie Smith

Christ's Fragrance

Our lives are a Christ-like fragrance rising up to God.
But this fragrance is perceived differently by those who
are being saved and by those who are perishing.
To those who are perishing, we are a dreadful
smell of death and doom. But to those who
are being saved, we are a life-giving perfume.

2 Corinthians 2:15–16 NLT

Though new scents come out on the market all the time, perfume is as old as the hills. Literally, for thousands of years, people have produced fragrances because of the demand. Humans like to smell nice things! For whatever reason, God wired our brains to remember and respond to smells in a way unlike any of the other senses.

Since we are made in God's image, it isn't that surprising to discover that God likes to smell good things too. Only, He isn't interested in what we can buy in the stores. God is sniffing out the Spirit of Christ in His children!

When you pray, God breathes it in. When you rejoice in His goodness, it deepens the aroma. When you love God and others, you have become a dispenser of Christ's exclusive fragrance. God detects His Son in you, and it pleases Him to no end.

Your divine fragrance floats beyond heaven. Its familiar scent strengthens the believers around you. And its lure draws the lost to its source.

Thank you for loving Jesus like you do. Everywhere you go, you fill the world with the beautiful aroma of Christ and His love.

Your name is like perfume poured out.
Song of Songs 1:3 NIV

The colored sunsets and starry heavens, the beautiful mountains and the shining seas, the fragrant woods and painted flowers, are not half so beautiful as a soul that is serving Jesus out of love.
Frederick W. Faber

Trust Steadily

Truly my soul finds rest in God;
my salvation comes from him.
Truly he is my rock and my salvation;
he is my fortress, I will never be shaken....
My salvation and my honor depend on God;
he is my mighty rock, my refuge.
Trust in him at all times, you people;
pour out your hearts to him,
for God is our refuge....
One thing God has spoken,
two things have I heard:
"Power belongs to you, God,
and with you, Lord, is unfailing love."

Psalm 62:1–2,7–8,11–12 NIV

Rest in the LORD, and wait patiently for Him.

Psalm 37:7 NKJV

Trust in the LORD with all your heart,
And lean not on your own understanding;
In all your ways acknowledge Him,
And He shall direct your paths.

Proverbs 3:5–6 NKJV

Trust steadily in God, hope unswervingly, love extravagantly.
And the best of the three is love.

1 Corinthians 13:13 MSG

*Infinite and yet personal, personal and yet infinite,
God may be trusted because He is the True One. He is
true, He acts truly, and He speaks truly.... Truthfulness
is therefore foundational for His trustworthiness.*

Os Guinness

Steadfast Love

The steadfast love of the LORD never ceases,
his mercies never come to an end;
they are new every morning;
great is your faithfulness.

Lamentations 3:22–23 ESV

Give thanks to the LORD, for he is good,
for his steadfast love endures forever.
Give thanks to the God of gods,
for his steadfast love endures forever.
Give thanks to the Lord of lords,
for his steadfast love endures forever;
to him who alone does great wonders,
for his steadfast love endures forever.

Psalm 136:1–4 ESV

Know that the LORD, He is God;
It is He who has made us, and not we ourselves;
We are His people and the sheep of His pasture.
Enter into His gates with thanksgiving,
And into His courts with praise.
Be thankful to Him, and bless His name.
For the LORD is good;
His mercy is everlasting,
And His truth endures to all generations.

Psalm 100:3–5 NKJV

All the paths of the LORD are steadfast love and faithfulness,
for those who keep his covenant and his testimonies.

Psalm 25:10 ESV

*You will never be able to count all of God's thoughts
toward you! You are loved beyond all knowing.*

Jan Silvious

All That He Has Done

Bless the LORD, O my soul,
And forget none of His benefits;
Who pardons all your iniquities,
Who heals all your diseases;
Who redeems your life from the pit,
Who crowns you with lovingkindness and compassion;
Who satisfies your years with good things,
So that your youth is renewed like the eagle....
The LORD is compassionate and gracious,
Slow to anger and abounding in lovingkindness....
For as high as the heavens are above the earth,
So great is His lovingkindness toward those who fear Him.
As far as the east is from the west,
So far has He removed our transgressions from us.
Just as a father has compassion on his children,
So the LORD has compassion on those who fear Him.

Psalm 103:2–5, 8, 11–13 NASB

Our days on earth are like grass;
like wildflowers, we bloom and die.
The wind blows, and we are gone—
as though we had never been here.
But the love of the LORD remains forever
with those who fear him.

Psalm 103:15–17 NLT

I pray for a lot of things. I pray that
I would always remain thankful.
I pray Thanksgiving whenever I get the opportunity.
I try to remember things that I've been blessed
with that I don't ever want to take for granted.

Mandisa

Secret of Abundant Life

Live generously.... Ask yourself what you want people to do
for you; then grab the initiative and do it for them! If you
only love the lovable, do you expect a pat on the back?...
I tell you, love your enemies. Help and give without
expecting a return. You'll never—I promise—regret it.
Live out this God-created identity the way our Father lives
toward us, generously and graciously.

Luke 6:30–33, 35 msg

Give generously...and do so without a grudging heart; then
because of this the LORD your God will bless you in all your
work and in everything you put your hand to.

Deuteronomy 15:10 NIV

Give, and it will be given to you. A good measure,
pressed down, shaken together and running over,
will be poured into your lap. For with the measure
you use, it will be measured to you.

Luke 6:38 NIV

Without question, the person who has the power to give a
blessing is greater than the one who is blessed.

Hebrews 7:7 NLT

*To love by freely giving is its own reward.
To be possessed by love and to in turn give love
away is to find the secret of abundant life.*

Gloria Gaither

Together Forever

I am convinced that nothing can ever separate us from God's love. Neither death nor life, neither angels nor demons, neither our fears for today nor our worries about tomorrow—not even the powers of hell can separate us from God's love.

Romans 8:38 NLT

It's why parents panic when they can't find their kids. Why lovers give each other rings and make lasting promises. Why people get so sad when someone dies.

People were created to stay together. We never want to lose the ones who are closest to us. But in a world riddled with the effects of sin, separation happens in a myriad of ways. Heartbreaking loss, time and again, hurts enough to make you pull back. To convince you not to put yourself out there any more. To choose no love at all instead of love at risk of loss.

Dear friend, bring your wounds to Jesus. Even He wept at the loss of his close friend, Lazarus. He knows separation hurts. Let him wipe the tears from your eyes and comfort you with His own faithful presence. Then reflect on His outstanding promise to you: nothing can separate you from the love of God in Christ Jesus! Just to drive the point home in Romans 8, Paul lists out a host of dramatic events that under normal circumstances would certainly tear people apart. But God's love is greater than anything else in creation. And by His power, He will always keep you close to Him, *no matter what!* Let God's promise of unfailing love strengthen your weary soul so you can keep living full and large, risking your all for the sake of His love.

I give them eternal life, and they shall never perish; no one will snatch them out of my hand.

John 10:28 NIV

Dare to love and to be a real friend.
The love you give and receive is a reality that
will lead you closer and closer to God as well as to
those whom God has given you to love.

Henri J. M. Nouwen

A Powerful Reminder

Praise the LORD!
I will thank the LORD with all my heart
as I meet with his godly people.
How amazing are the deeds of the LORD!
All who delight in him should ponder them.
Everything he does reveals his glory and majesty.
His righteousness never fails.
He causes us to remember his wonderful works.
How gracious and merciful is our LORD!
He gives food to those who fear him;
he always remembers his covenant.
He has shown his great power to his people....
All he does is just and good,
and all his commandments are trustworthy.
They are forever true,
to be obeyed faithfully and with integrity.
He has paid a full ransom for his people.
He has guaranteed his covenant with them forever.
What a holy, awe-inspiring name he has!
Fear of the LORD is the foundation of true wisdom.
All who obey his commandments will grow in wisdom.

Psalm 111:1–10 NLT

When we keep in mind the amazing grace poured out on us, our hearts are stirred to share God's grace with others. Radiant women, we are His messengers, His ambassadors, and the proclaimers entrusted with the good news of salvation.

Marian Jordan

Traveling Companions

How blessed all those in whom you live,
whose lives become roads you travel;
They wind through lonesome valleys, come upon brooks,
discover cool springs and pools brimming with rain!
God-traveled, these roads curve up the mountain, and
at the last turn—Zion! God in full view!

Psalm 84:5–7 MSG

If I take the wings of the dawn,
If I dwell in the remotest part of the sea,
Even there Your hand will lead me,
And Your right hand will lay hold of me.

Psalm 139:9–10 NASB

A day in your courts is better than a thousand elsewhere.
I would rather be a doorkeeper in the house of my God
than dwell in the tents of wickedness.
For the Lᴏʀᴅ God is a sun and shield;
the Lᴏʀᴅ bestows favor and honor.
No good thing does he withhold
from those who walk uprightly.
O Lᴏʀᴅ of hosts,
blessed is the one who trusts in you!

Psalm 84:10–12 ᴇsᴠ

*It is God to whom and with whom we travel,
and while He is the End of our journey,
He is also at every stopping place.*

Elisabeth Elliot

Blessings to Empower

When I think of all this, I fall to my knees and pray to the
Father, the Creator of everything in heaven and on earth.
I pray that from his glorious, unlimited resources he will
empower you with inner strength through his Spirit. Then
Christ will make his home in your hearts as you trust in him.
Your roots will grow down into God's love and keep you
strong. And may you have the power to understand,
as all God's people should, how wide, how long, how high,
and how deep his love is. May you experience the love
of Christ, though it is too great to understand fully.
Then you will be made complete with all the fullness
of life and power that comes from God.

Now all glory to God, who is able, through his mighty power
at work within us, to accomplish infinitely more than we
might ask or think. Glory to him in the church and in Christ
Jesus through all generations forever and ever! Amen.

Ephesians 3:14–21 NLT

God often calls us to do things that we do not have the ability to do. Spiritual discernment is knowing if God calls you to do something, God empowers you to do it.

Suzanne Farnham

Drink Deeply

All praise to God, the Father of our Lord Jesus Christ,
who has blessed us with every spiritual blessing in the
heavenly realms because we are united with Christ. Even
before he made the world, God loved us and chose us
in Christ to be holy and without fault in his eyes. God
decided in advance to adopt us into his own family by
bringing us to himself through Jesus Christ. This is what
he wanted to do, and it gave him great pleasure. So we
praise God for the glorious grace he has poured out on us
who belong to his dear Son. He is so rich in kindness and
grace that he purchased our freedom with the blood of his
Son and forgave our sins. He has showered his kindness
on us, along with all wisdom and understanding.

Ephesians 1:2–8 NLT

Jesus stood and said..., "Let anyone who is thirsty
come to me and drink. Whoever believes in me,
as Scripture has said, rivers of living water
will flow from within them."

John 7:37–38 NIV

*We must drink deeply from the very Source
the deep calm and peace of interior quietude
and refreshment of God, allowing the pure
water of divine grace to flow plentifully
and unceasingly from the Source itself.*

Mother Teresa

Battle Gear

*We are not fighting against flesh-and-blood enemies,
but against evil rulers and authorities of the unseen
world.... Therefore, put on every piece of God's armor
so you will be able to resist the enemy.*

Ephesians 6:12–13 NLT

Every morning you roll out of bed and head to the bath-
room. Yes, there it is, the mirror with your disheveled
reflection in it. Already you know the drill: Brush teeth, take
a shower, find an outfit, fix your hair, and brace yourself for
the day's tasks you can already hear calling your name.

One of those voices you hear, though—the still, small,
quiet one—is God's Spirit vying for your attention. It seems
that in the tyranny of the urgent or the monotony of the
seemingly mundane, you've forgotten the true state of affairs.
When you rise to face another day, you're stepping back into
a spiritual battle raging around you. God warns you that the
unseen forces of evil bent on your destruction stand ready to
attack and drag you to the ground. Without proper protection, your mind and spirit won't stand a chance.

The commander of heaven's armies, Jesus Himself, has
given you the spiritual armor you need to win the day's
battle. The belt of truth, breastplate of righteousness, shoes

of peace, shield of faith, helmet of salvation, and the sword of the Spirit are each designed to not only protect you, but empower you to take down enemy strongholds by God's Spirit. Each piece is a part of your relationship with Jesus who is your defender and Savior. Take time today to strengthen yourself in Him. Clothe yourself with His presence, and take on the day with a new determination—victory and glory in Christ!

I have fought the good fight. I have finished the race. I have kept the faith.

2 Timothy 4:7 NIV

You can fight with confidence where you are sure of victory. With Christ and for Christ victory is certain.

St. Bernard of Clairvaux

Strong to the End

May God our Father
and the Lord Jesus Christ
give you grace and peace.
I always thank my God for you and
for the gracious gifts he has given you....
He will keep you strong to the end
so that you will be free
from all blame on the day
when our Lord Jesus Christ returns.
God will do this, for he
is faithful to do what he says,
and he has invited you into partnership
with his Son, Jesus Christ our Lord.

1 Corinthians 1:3–4, 8–9 NLT

Finally, be strong in the Lord and in his mighty power....
Put on the full armor of God, so that when the day of evil
comes, you may be able to stand your ground,
and after you have done everything, to stand.

Ephesians 6:10, 13 NIV

Now may our Lord Jesus Christ himself,
and God our Father, who loved us and gave us eternal
comfort and good hope through grace, comfort your hearts
and establish them in every good work and word.

2 Thessalonians 2:16–17 ESV

*Taken separately, the experiences of life can
work harm and not good. Taken together,
they make a pattern of blessing and strength
the like of which the world does not know.*

V. Raymond Edman

WOMEN OF JOY™

The world moves so fast, sometimes you need a little time
to break away. Our friends at Women of Joy have been
encouraging women with the Word of God, the joy of
music, and the spirit of friendship through Women of
Joy Weekends for more than a decade. Offering teaching
and worship, with time for fun sprinkled in, you will be
amazed at what a difference forty-eight hours with a group
of women, friends, or daughters can make.
Visit www.womenofjoy.org for more information.

...inspired by life
EllieClaire.com

At Ellie Claire® Gift & Paper Expressions, we are
passionate about living life beyond the ordinary. We
invite you to use our products to express your thoughts,
record your prayers, embrace your dreams, and find
encouragement in a life inspired by joy. Discover more
Ellie Claire journals, devotionals, and gift books at
EllieClaire.com.